GUIDE TO BROKER PRICE OPINION SUCCESS

Real Estate Agents: Learn How to Earn Thousands of Dollars a Month with BPOs

BPO Training Manual

ALLISON ROBBINS

abbott press

Abbott Press books may be ordered through booksellers or by contacting:

Abbott Press
1663 Liberty Drive
Bloomington, IN 47403
www.abbottpress.com
Phone: 1 (866) 697-5310

ISBN: 978-1-4582-1858-2 (sc)
ISBN: 978-1-4582-1859-9 (e)

Library of Congress Control Number: 2015901177

Print information available on the last page.

Abbott Press rev. date: 03/04/2015

ATTENTION AGENTS

In today's market, only the innovative survive. That's why as real estate agents we need to be able to use all sources of income available within our market. **BPOs (Broker Price Opinions) are a great way to generate that extra income or even become a full time BPO agent and watch the cash stack up.**

Are you new to real estate? Are you tired of getting leads that never pan out? Tired of driving clients around to 20 houses before they decide not to buy? Has your real estate business been decimated by the foreclosures on the market? Have you put your license on inactive status until the market changes? In real estate, only the strong survive. **If you have been doing the same thing and yielding poor results, maybe it's time to try something new.** Just ask yourself one question…. Do I make what I deserve? After you answer that question, there is only one thing left to ponder…. **Am I ready to start making the income I deserve?**

The key to becoming a successful money making machine in the bpo industry is within this book. I will walk you through how to get business, how to maintain and grow business relationships with asset companies, and how to become a fully functional bpo producer that can yield more than 10,000 in monthly revenue. Consider this… **Most agents would have to sell 2-4 houses a month in today's market to generate the income that I make in BPOs in one month**. Here is the kicker, **I don't**

even work 8 hours a day, and I have every weekend to spend with my family.

BPOs are guaranteed money, with very little expenditures, checks paid to you on a monthly basis and they become something to depend on in today's market. So even if you are still prospecting for clients to list or sell homes to, the bottom line is that BPOs can become that extra income you have been looking for and help you stay abreast on local market activity in the process. As real estate agents, we need to focus on our IPAs, (Income Producing Activities) so it's time to focus on the untapped income you could be making doing bpos.

CONTENTS

Chapter 1

WHAT IS A BROKER PRICE OPINION??

What is a BPO?

A BPO or Broker Price Opinion is a tool that is often used by lenders, homeowners, and investment companies to determine current value of a property in the current market conditions. It allows the homeowner to get a current value and compare it to the mortgage balance, so they may find solutions or have up to date data on the property. Some reasons a BPO may be ordered could be a loan refinance, delinquent payments, pending foreclosure, short sale price/offer verification or to determine potential resale and current market value.

They often times rely on brokers and agents to value the properties because sometimes the expense and delay of an appraisal is unnecessary. The order comes in from an asset company and is requiring the agent to do a drive by bpo or interior bpo. The drive by bpo only requires photos from the exterior of the home, while the interior requires both exterior and interior photos of the home. At the time the order is assigned, they will also advise the agent if they are looking for a distressed value, fair market value or rehabbed value of a property.

The bpo is in essence a market summary report and a CMA, which we as real estate agents all know how to do. You must know your market area and then find three active listings and three sold listings to support the current value of the home in question. If you are unfamiliar with performing CMAs this training manual will show you in detail exactly what the bpo companies are looking for in their BPOs.

It is crucial that you check your own state laws regarding BPOs to determine if you can do them. Also, you must speak with your broker to ensure that they do not want a cut of the bpo payments. Most brokers do not require you to split it with them, so the money is all yours.

You must comply with all federal and state laws governing bpo practices. To be able to take BPO assignments you have to have a valid active license for the state in which the bpo is being assigned. It is also imperative that you have the ability to search the property and comparable properties within your MLS board database and tax record database. If you know a city is not in your system, do not accept the order. Also, you must commit to personally visiting and photographing the home, this cannot be outsourced or compromised at all.

A BPO is only to be done by a licensed agent, you have to personally pull the comps and complete the form with adjustments and pricing. Some agents use data entry specialist to enter the comparable information but the bottom line is that you are responsible for all information in the report and if incorrect, you will be the one to answer to the discrepancies.

There are many different types of services that can be requested by BPO companies for agents to complete. The prices for each bpo will range in value depending on the type of report the customer wants. Below are basic types of reports or valuations that BPO companies assign to agents.

Interior BPO:

✓ Description: BPO includes a narrative on local market conditions, neighborhood characteristics, subject property condition, analysis of three current sold and three current listings with photos. Suggested list and sales price based on repaired and as is value. Exterior photos of home and all internal rooms with noted repairs and repair estimates.

Exterior BPO:

✓ Description: BPO includes a narrative on local market conditions, neighborhood characteristics, subject property condition, analysis of three current sold and three current listings with photos. Suggested list and sales price based on repaired and as is value. Exterior photos of home.

Desk Reviews:

✓ Description: BPO includes a narrative on local market conditions, neighborhood characteristics, subject property condition, analysis of three current sold and three current listings with photos. Suggested list and sales price based on repaired and as is value.

Rental Addendums:

✓ Description: Rental Addendum includes a narrative on local rental market conditions, neighborhood characteristics, subject property condition, analysis of with two leased comps and two active comps with suggested rental value.

Inspections:

✓ Description: Interior and exterior property inspection noting all repairs and repair estimates with photos of exterior and all interior of home including photos of noted repairs.

LIST OF MATERIALS NEEDED FOR BPO WORK

List of Materials Needed for BPO work:

- **Camera** (No less than 580 pixels.) Set camera to have accurate time and date stamp on the photos, this is a requirement for some bpo companies.
- **GPS Navigator system** – any type of system that can get you from point A to point B with turn by turn directions.
- **Routing Software** – when doing more than 10 BPOs in a day, I recommend using routing software to ensure an efficient route.
- **Car** – the car is going to get a lot of miles of wear and tear. I recommend the car be gas efficient because this job requires a lot of gas, and you always want to minimize your expenses.
- **Computer with internet access** – this is imperative that you have internet access and are able to work at a steady pace on your computer. 80% of this job is done right in front of your computer. You need a comfortable work space set aside.
- **Cell Phone–** this will come in handy because interior bpo's often times require you to call agents or home owners to set up a time to go take the photos. Having a cell phone handy is imperative to success within this industry, to make contact with agents, receive solicitation emails and for safety.

Quick thought on Safety:

As a realtor, safety has to be a top priority. How often do we find ourselves in situations that we second guess our safety? Vacant homes, first meets with new clients, or flat tires on the side of a road? We need to be cautious, and take measures to protect our own safety. If we don't, no one else will.

Here are some tips for agents to keep safe as we work:

- Use your own common sense and follow your personal instincts.
- Carry a whistle, mace or pepper spray.
- Park in well-lit areas.
- Always tell someone at the office of where and with whom your bpos will be.
- Keep your car well-maintained to avoid breaking down in remote areas.
- Have a cell phone on you at all times.

3

TIPS FOR RECEIVING WORK FROM BPO COMPANIES

Tips for receiving work from BPO Companies:

Register with the companies

The first step is finding companies to work for and submitting your name and information to become a vendor with the company. Go online to search for a free list of BPO providers. After you obtain or create a list of companies to register with you are now ready to research each company and submit to them your application to work with them. Go to each company website to see how they accept applications. There are different ways to register depending on the company, some companies require you to email them, others want you to call, and most of them have forms that you can fill out online. Some have their own applications that you must print and fax back. Whatever the case may be, make sure to follow through. Keep track of every company you sign up with and any user name/password you obtain. After you register with these companies, you must make sure to upload or fax (depending on their individual requirements) copies of the following documentation:

- Updated E and O insurance form (you can get this from your Broker)
- Copy of Real Estate License or Pocket Card
- W-9 Form

Make Contact:

This is extremely important. You have already put your name in their system, provided all documentation needed and now you are ready to get some work. Make it a point to reach out and call or email the company to determine who is in charge of assigning orders in your state. Be sure to get their email address and/or phone number. You will need to call and/or email them to introduce yourself, tell them the area you work specifically and make sure to tell them you would greatly appreciate any work they could send your way. Don't give up until you make contact.

Be Patient

For most of us, the bpos will not come pouring in right away. Just like other careers, you do have to work your way up with most companies to reach your maximum potential. This means that you might only be getting a few orders a week to start off. The key to becoming successful in this industry is to do the work you get with quality and to keep accepting them as much as possible. Many bpo companies are set up to send out email alerts when there is an available order in your area. This can sometimes mean that you are in a race to be the first to accept the order. It is recommended that you have a cell phone capable of immediate email access such as an iPhone or android phone. You will need to adjust your POP settings to get your emails sent to you as quickly as possible.

Always remember that the company is looking for a job well done. Here are three key concepts that all bpo companies look for with a bpo vendor:

- Accuracy
- Turnaround Time
- Quality

In the long run, the bpo company that you are getting work from is going to want to see you representing them well. This means % QC approved, volume and turnaround time play a key role in your quality score. You must remember these companies are submitting your analysis to their clients, so they want to see complete sentences and thorough comments regarding the subject property. Occasionally you may receive a "kickback" or "clarification request" there is a chapter in this book entitled "How to address a kickback" for further instruction on this situation. The bottom line is, yes there will be some mistakes, but you have to make it your goal to do the best possible to deliver a quality product. Put it in your head that the bpo company is your customer, and their clients are your customer as well. Please be aware that your success in this industry is determined by their satisfaction with your work.

MAINTAINING CONTACT WITH BPO PROVIDERS

Maintaining Contact with BPO Providers:

Most bpo companies have people that work directly with your state or area assigning orders; the key is to find the names of these people and attempt to make contact with them. This is a somewhat aggressive approach to getting bpo solicitations, but it works. I'm not saying that you have to do this by any means, you will still get work. This is a step to go the extra mile to attempt to get more work in a shorter amount of time.

Recommendations:

- Create an email account specifically for BPO solicitations and BPO contact with providers.
- Have each BPO company identify your point of contact; some companies have one point of contact per state.
- Send an email to your point of contact to introduce yourself or give them a call. Tell them the areas you work and let them know that you pride yourself on quick turnaround times and quality work. Ask for any orders they can send your way and let them know how much you appreciate it.

Tips for maintaining contact with BPO companies:

There is going to be a point when you have signed up with many companies. It is not humanly possible to remember all the companies, web addresses or login information.

Create a list that you can reference to with the company name, their website address, their phone numbers, point of contact email address and your login information. You can print this out and keep it right next to your computer for easy access.

When a bpo company tries to contact you, regarding updates on order submissions or revisions requested it is imperative that you respond to that email or phone call as soon as possible. This needs to be done within hours of getting the contact. Don't put this on the backburner. I have worked with many agents over the years that saw a decline in their work. They went from being successful in bpos to not successful at all. In all those cases, it was apparent that they let their bpo work fall to the side. They were not responsive with the companies, they were turning their orders in late and the companies eventually quit sending them work. Some agents will try to juggle prospecting with these bpo orders, and this can be done. However, you must realize that you have to prioritize a lot of your work time to bpos to truly bring in big revenue.

Never Stop Prospecting:

It is vital to continue to sign up with new companies as they come on the market. You never know who will be getting large amounts of work in the future. So have your name in with as many companies as possible. If you hear or read about a new company, sign up with them immediately.

Chapter

5

CLIENT
INSTRUCTIONS

Client Instructions

Search Parameters:

Read the Instructions on the BPO request. This is very important because some clients put weight on certain search parameters more than others. For example, one company may want comps within one mile and they would rather sacrifice getting comps that are unlike the subject property characteristics but within one mile radius as opposed to similar comparables past one mile of subject property.

BPOs are ordered for different reasons, so the client instructions section of the bpo is very important. Does the client want a fair market value or a distressed value? Do they mind if you use short sales or foreclosure properties for comparables? What kind of marketing time does the client have in mind? If you don't know the answers to these questions, you can't do the bpo correctly...

Understand what the client is asking for is key to your success within the industry. This is also a time saving tip that will prevent you from having to redo reports because you didn't read the instructions and give the client what they were looking for the first time.

There are bpo standards that go over all standard search parameters for finding comparable properties, but at the end of the day the clients request come before these standards and should be treated as priority.

Photo Instructions:

Different photos may also be requested from the client, so make sure to read the photo requirements to see exactly how many photos need to be taken of the subject property.

Interior Access:

Directions in the client instructions also give you contact or access information for your interior orders. Some companies may put access information, such as a lockbox combo or supra access info. Some companies put a name and contact number for you to get a hold of to gain access to the home.

Conduct while taking the Photo:

Other requirements include what the client expects out of you while taking the photos. If the photo is an exterior, they ask that you not have any contact with the homeowner. That means you have to be discrete while taking the photos. Also, you should not step on their property while the photo is being taken; this needs to be done from the street.

Please remember to give each tenant/homeowner great customer service and make the experience pleasant. Every person involved in this process is a customer of another customer. Meaning, the little fish are just as important as the big fish. You are a reflection of your brokerage, the asset company, the bank and the industry.

Chapter

6

HOW TO DO A BPO

BPO Basics:

It is very important to use correct grammar and spelling in the report. This is a professional analysis and should look like it from top to bottom. That means no all caps in your comment section, no misspelled words and looking professional. Also, refrain from using first person while writing comments into the bpo, such as "I'. For example, instead of saying "I expanded my search parameters" use "expanded search parameters" All comments made should be objective and should be worded and expressed in a way that stays in line with the provisions of the Fair Housing Act.

Comparable search should be focused on time and distance. Comps older than 6 months should not be used in a BPO report. Comp search should not go past .5 miles for urban locations, 1 mile for suburban and 5 miles for rural. If these parameters have to be expanded, a comment will need to be made within the report stating what circumstances led to having to expand out of the normal parameters. It's best to start your comparable search in the same subdivision or immediate area of the subject property. Then start filtering your search in MLS by square footage, year built and lot size.

All comps selected should be within the same geographical boundaries. For example, picking comps on the other side of the interstate or highway could affect and skew the value you are giving the subject property. Pick the sales and listings that are most comparable to the subject property in condition, quality, design and physical characteristics. Please keep in mind the client instructions and if they are wanting distressed or fair market values, this should steer you to pick the same type of comparable properties to support your bpo with the final value conclusion. You must attempt to bracket your comp characteristics against that of the subjects. So if possible, make an attempt to find a comp with smaller sq ft than subject and one with larger sq ft of subject. Bracket sq footage, lot size and year built. If this is not possible due to lack of comps, then you would need to make comments in the comment section to explain why you were unable to bracket square foot, lot size and age.

How to do a BPO:

Locate Subject Property Information:

- RF # or Tax ID number:
- Attached or detached?
- County
- Land value:
- Taxes:
- Sold Date:
- Last Sold Amount:
- Subdivision:
- Stories:
- Property characteristics: square footage, bed, bath, lot size, garage, basement, age

Locate comparable properties:

3 Sold Comparables:

- Sold within past 4-6 months
- Similar to subject physical characteristics
- Within one mile of Subject
- In same school district as subject

3 Active Comparables:

- Listed within the past year
- Similar to subject physical characteristics

- Within one mile of Subject
- In same school district as subject

Search parameters should not be expanded past 30% variance from subject property. For example, if the subject was built in 1994, you would not want to use a comparable that was built in 1976. You want at most 10 year gap between comparable age and subject age.

The following characteristics should not exceed subject's characteristics by 30% variance:

- Age (+/- 10 Years)
- Lot size (+ / - 2 Acres)
- Square footage (+/- 300 sq ft)
- Sales price or list price vs. current value of subject property (30-40 grand)

Save the Comparable Photos:

After selecting comparables, make sure to save a picture of each one to your computer. Many bpos require you to upload photos of comparables that you used.

Enter Data into Report:

Enter all data into BPO form, make adjustments for differences between subject and comparable properties.

Price the Home:

Price the home to reflect as is value and repaired value of home

Upload Photos:

You will upload required photos of the subject property and comparable properties to the BPO form.

RESIDENTIAL BROKER PRICE OPINION

REO# _____ This BPO is the ☐ Initial ☐ 2nd Opinion ☐ Updated ☐ Extr. Only DATE _____

PROPERTY ADDRESS: _____   SALES REPRESENTATIVE: _____

_____   CLIENT NAME _____

FIRM NAME: _____   COMPLETED BY _____

PHONE NO. _____   FAX NO. _____

EMAIL ADDR: _____

I. GENERAL MARKET CONDITIONS

Current market conditions: ☐ Depressed ☐ Slow ☐ Stable ☐ Improving ☐ Excellent

Employment conditions: ☐ Declining ☐ Stable ☐ Improving

Market price of this type property has: ☐ Decreased ____ % in past ____ months

☐ Increased ____ % in past ____ months

☐ Remained Stable.

Estimated percentage of owners vs. tenants in neighborhood: ____% owner occupant ____% tenant

There is a: ☐ normal supply ☐ over supply ☐ shortage of comparable listings in the neighborhood.

Approximate number of comparable units for sale in neighborhood:

No. of competing listings in neighborhood that are REO or Corporate owned: _____

No. of boarded or blocked-up homes: _____

II. SUBJECT MARKETABILITY

Range of values in the neighborhood is $ _____ to $ _____ .

The subject is an ☐ over improvement ☐ under improvement ☐ appropriate improvement for the neighborhood.

Normal marketing time in the area is _____ days.

Are all types of financing available for the property? ☐ Yes ☐ No If no,explain _____

Has the property been on the market in the last 12 months? ☐ Yes ☐ No If yes, $ _____ list price (attach MLS printout)

To the best of your knowledge, why did it not sell? _____

Unit Type: ☐ single family detached ☐ condo ☐ co-op ☐ mobile home

☐ single family attached ☐ townhouse ☐ modular ☐ condotel

If condo/other mandatory associations exist:Fee $ _____ monthly or ☐ annually. Current? ☐ Yes ☐ No Fee delinquent$ _____

The fee includes: ☐ Insurance ☐ Landscape ☐ Pool ☐ Tennis Other _____

Association Contact: Name: _____   Phone No.: _____

III. COMPETITIVE CLOSED SALES

ITEM	SUBJECT	COMPARABLE NUMBER 1		COMPARABLE NUMBER 2		COMPARABLE NUMBER 3	
Address							
Proximity to Subject		REO/CORP ☐		REO/CORP ☐		REO/CORP ☐	
Sale Price	$	$		$		$	
Price/Gross Living Area	$ Sq.Ft.	$ Sq.Ft.		$ Sq.Ft.		$ Sq.Ft.	
Data Source							
Sale Date & Days on Market							
VALUE ADJUSTMENTS	DESCRIPTION	DESCRIPTION	+(-) Adjustment	DESCRIPTION	+(-) Adjustment	DESCRIPTION	+(-) Adjustment
Sales or Financing Concessions							
Location							
Leasehold/Fee Simple							
Site							
View							
Design and Appeal							
Quality of Construction							
Year Built							
Condition							
Above Grade Room Count	Total Bdrms Baths	Total Bdrms Baths		Total Bdrms Baths		Total Bdrms Baths	
Gross Living Area	Sq. Ft.	Sq. Ft.		Sq. Ft.		Sq. Ft.	
Basement & Finished Rooms Below Grade							
Functional Utility							
Heating/Cooling							
Energy Efficient Items							
Garage/Carport							
Porches, Patio, Deck							
Fireplace(s), etc.							
Fence, Pool, etc.							
Other							
Net Adj. (total)		☐ + ☐ - $		☐ + ☐ - $		☐ + ☐ - $	
Adjusted Sales Price of Comparable		$		$		$	

REO# _____

IV. MARKETING STRATEGY

☐ As-Is ☐ Minimal Lender Required Repairs ☐ Repaired   Most Likely Buyer: ☐ Owner occupant ☐ Investor

V. REPAIRS

Itemize ALL repairs needed to bring property from its present "as is" condition to average marketable condition for the neighborhood, EVEN IF you selected an "As Is" marketing strategy. Check the box next to the repair ONLY if you recommend that we perform the repair for most successful marketing of the property, or leave check box blank if not recommending.

☐	_____ $ _____	☐	_____ $ _____
☐	_____ $ _____	☐	_____ $ _____
☐	_____ $ _____	☐	_____ $ _____
☐	_____ $ _____	☐	_____ $ _____
☐	_____ $ _____	☐	_____ $ _____

GRAND TOTAL FOR ALL REPAIRS $ _____

VI. COMPETITIVE LISTINGS

ITEM	SUBJECT	COMPARABLE NUMBER 1		COMPARABLE NUMBER 2		COMPARABLE NUMBER 3	
Address							
Proximity to Subject			REO/CORP ☐		REO/CORP ☐		REO/CORP ☐
List Price	$	$		$		$	
Price/Gross Living Area	$ /Sq.Ft.	$ /Sq.Ft.		$ /Sq.Ft.		$ /Sq.Ft.	
Data Source							
VALUE ADJUSTMENTS	DESCRIPTION	DESCRIPTION	+(-) Adjustment	DESCRIPTION	+(-) Adjustment	DESCRIPTION	+(-) Adjustment
Sales or Financing Concessions							
Days on Market							
Location							
Leasehold/Fee Simple							
Site							
View							
Design and Appeal							
Quality of Construction							
Year Built							
Condition							
Above Grade Room Count	Total Bdrms Baths	Total Bdrms Baths		Total Bdrms Baths		Total Bdrms Baths	
Gross Living Area	Sq. Ft.	Sq. Ft.		Sq. Ft.		Sq. Ft.	
Basement & Finished Rooms Below Grade							
Functional Utility							
Heating/Cooling							
Energy Efficient Items							
Garage/Carport							
Porches, Patio, Deck Fireplace(s), etc.							
Fence, Pool, etc.							
Other							
Net Adj. (total)		☐+ ☐- $		☐+ ☐- $		☐+ ☐- $	
Adjusted Sales Price of Comparable		$		$		$	

VII. THE MARKET VALUE

(The value must fall within the range indicated by the adjusted Sales Price of the Comparables. Place the most weight on those comparables that are recent, in closest proximity, and with the fewest overall adjustments. Never average values.)

	Market Value	Suggested List Price
AS IS	$ _____	$ _____
REPAIRED	$ _____	$ _____

VIII. COMMENTS ☐

(Include specific positives / negatives, special concerns, encroachments, easements, water rights, environmental concerns, flood zones, etc. Check the box if additional comments are continued in Case Comments in AMN or on Page 3 of this report.)

_____

_____

_____

_____

_____

_____

_____

Signature: _____   Date: _____

Residential Broker Price Opinion Breakdown

A broker price opinion has many sections to fill as you complete the report to entirety. Please note, every question or blank on this form must be completed in order to submit this to the client. If you don't know the answer to a question on the form, you must stop and go find the answer by online research. Let's look at each common section and discuss what is required to complete the order to satisfaction of your clients.

I. General Market Conditions

This section requires you to be abreast of the market trends and conditions within the area of the subject property. You can use tools such as your local MLS, Zillow or Realtor websites to determine the general market conditions for the area and deliver an accurate report. General Market conditions require you to know if the current market is stable, slow or improving within the area. Also you must know the % of increase or decrease the market has had within a specific time frame. It also requires you to be abreast of the current employment conditions within the area. Also, supply and demand should be covered within this section, is there a normal supply of homes, oversupply or shortage of comparable listings in the neighborhood. Pull up your MLS to determine the approximate number of comparable listings for sale in the neighborhood and be prepared to list the number of competing listings in the neighborhood that area REO and corporate owned as well as how many boarded up or blocked up homes are within the area.

II. Subject Marketability

This section requires you to zoom in on the subject property in terms of marketability of the home. Listing the range of values within the area is important and that information can be obtained from your local MLS. Subject marketability also covers the improvement of the home versus those in the area, is it an over improvement, under improvement or appropriate improvement for the area. Normal marketing time for the area is also important information to subject marketability. You must know if all financing is available for the property and if the property has been on the market for the past 12 months. This is important information and must be included in your report and in strategy to price the home. If a home recently expired on the market at a specific price, you would probably not want to price it higher than the expired price on your value conclusion. If the home recently sold, you would probably not want to price it less than what it just sold for. If you have a valid reason and comps to support doing this, you can always make comments at the end of your report to validate your price conclusion. If they home did not sell while it was on the market within the last 12 months, the BPO asks you to hypothesize why you think the home did not sell. Subject marketability section also asks you to determine what type of unit the home is such as single family detached. Please note, whatever type of unit the property is, you must have all comps the same unit. For example, if you selected townhome, all comps should be townhomes as well. It will also require you to list any and all HOA Information for the subject property.

III. Competitive Sold Comps

In this section you will list the subject property characteristics on the first column. Then the following three columns will consist of your sold comparable that you have picked for the subject property. You should select the most recent sold comps and input all sale data into the BPO such as sale price, concessions and sale date. All comps should be within a mile of your subject property and be very similar to the subject characteristics of square foot, bed and bath count, lot size and year built. Condition and quality should be similar as well. For anything requiring adjustments, you will be able to list that amount next to each comparable needing adjustments and obtain a net adjustment to apply to your sales price.

IV. Marketing Strategy

This section requires you to select which method you think the home should sell best. Should it be sold as is or with repairs? Who is the most likely buyer? Is the home vacant or occupied? All of these questions will help determine the best method to sell the home.

V. Repairs

All repairs seen during inspection should be listed here and given a repair estimated amount next to each repair. The grand total of your repairs will be used during your pricing of the property.

VI. Competitive listings

This section you will see prefilled data for the subject property in the first column. Then the following three columns will consist of your listing or active comparables that you have selected for the subject property. You should select the most recent active comps and input all listing data into the BPO such as original list price, current list price and listing date. All comps should be within a mile of your subject property and be very similar to the subject characteristics of square foot, bed and bath count, lot size and year built. Condition and quality should be similar as well. For anything requiring adjustments, you will be able to list that amount next to each comparable needing adjustments and obtain a net adjustment to apply to your list prices.

VII. Market value

This section is where you price the home. AS IS and repaired values should be listed. They must all fall within the indicated value of the closed sales and current listings. AS IS would be the home priced with no repairs noted and Repaired is taking the as is price and adding the exact amount of repairs to the value. Please take note there is market value and list price required in this section.

VIII. Comments

This section allows you to make any pertinent disclosures or explanations of the report, property or comps used in the analysis. Comments are required within every BPO and avoid using the same comments every time you do an analysis. This is called "canned comments" and are frowned upon. Each BPO should have comments specific to the property, comps and search done for each BPO. You should also use this section to explain if any normal search parameters, such as age, square footage or distance were exceeded and why this was necessary.

IX. Photos

Photos of all comparables used in the report must be uploaded to the photo section. It is important to use the front view of each home to include in the report. No aerial views, interior room views or subdivision signs should be used for comparable photos. The clients need to get a visual of the homes you say are comparable to the subject. All subject photos will be uploaded here as well. Showing the front of the home, all sides, street scene and address verification to name a few.

7

MAKING ADJUSTMENTS

Making adjustments:

Adjustments: In a CMA or BPO, the increases or decreases to the sales price of a comparable property to arrive at an indicated value for the property being appraised. In an effort to make comparables and subject property similar.

*** Check with your broker regarding what the correct pricing for these adjustments within your specific market area.*

Adjustments may be made for several reasons such as:

- ✓ Seller concessions (–)
- ✓ Garage (+/–)
- ✓ Age (+/–)
- ✓ Sq ft (+/–)
- ✓ Lot size (+/–)
- ✓ Bedrooms (+/–)
- ✓ Bathrooms (+/–)
- ✓ Basements (+/–)

When doing adjustments remember that the subject property never gets deducted from. The subject is the basis for the adjustment, so look at and make adjustments to the comparable. If the comparable has more than subject, you would subtract from the comparable. If the comparable has less than the subject you would add to the comparable.

The idea is to get the comparable comp to mirror the subject and form a value based on that.

Please view this example

	SUBJECT			COMP 1			Adjustment	COMP 2			Adjustment	Comp 3			Adjustment
	Total	Beds	Baths	Total	Beds	Baths		Total	Beds	Baths		Total	Beds	Baths	
room count	5	3	2	7	5	4	-7000	6	3	2	0	7	4	2	-2000
GLA (sq ft)			1947			2624	-5000			2143	0			1672	0
Basement			819			1184	0			943	0			840	0
Total adjustment							-12000				0				-2000

Comments are needed regarding the differences between the subject versus comparable, especially when there is no space on the bpo form to make adjustments. If there is no space for adjustments, make sure that you mentally make adjustments to determine your final value conclusion. Each form will differ by company and product.

It is very important to remain consistent with your adjustments throughout the report.

Adjustments should never be applied in an effort to manipulate a property value or final value conclusion and should always be supported by the market, meaning adjustments should only be made to characteristics that are acknowledged by the market. Here is a list of characteristics that are typically acknowledged by the market.

*** Check with your broker regarding what the correct pricing for these adjustments within your specific market area.*

- ✓ Seller Concessions:
- ✓ Location:
- ✓ Lot size or site:
- ✓ View:
- ✓ Design and Appeal:
- ✓ Age:
- ✓ Quality of Construction:
- ✓ Room Count:
- ✓ Bed Count:

- ✓ Bath Count:
- ✓ Basement and finished below grade sq ft:
- ✓ Heating/Cooling:
- ✓ Garage/ Carport:
- ✓ Functional Utility:
- ✓ Porches:
- ✓ Patio:
- ✓ Fireplace:
- ✓ Fence:
- ✓ Pool:
- ✓ Amenities:

Example Adjustment Exercise:

	Sold 1		Sold 2		Sold 3	

	SUBJECT			COMP 1			Adjustment	COMP 2			Adjustment	Comp 3			Adjustment
	Total	Beds	Baths	Total	Beds	Baths		Total	Beds	Baths		Total	Beds	Baths	
room count	5	3	2	7	4	3	-3500	6	4	2	-2000	7	4	3	-3500
GLA (sq ft)			1947			1852	0			2668	-5000			1886	0
Basement			819			300	0			0	5000			822	0
Total adjustment							-3500				-2000				-3500

Example will be using the adjustment of

+/- 2000 for one bedroom
+/- 1500 for one bathroom
+/- 5000 for basement
+/- 5000 for sq ft

Sold 1: Sold comp 1 is similar to the subject, however it does have on more bed and one more bath than the subject property. So I will want to take one bed and one bath "away" from sold comp 1 to make it similar to the subject property.

Total deduction -2000 + -1500= -3500 total Net adjustment.

Sold 2: Sold comp 2 is similar to the subject however it does have one more bedroom than the subject, has larger sq ft and also does not have basement sq footage as the subject does. So I will take one bedroom out by subtracting -2000 take out sq footage -5000, I will add 5000 for a basement. (Give the comp a basement)

Total deduction -2000 + -5000 -5000= -2000 total Net adjustment.

Sold 3: Sold comp 3 is similar to the subject, however it does have on more bed and one more bath than the subject property. So I will want to take one bed and one bath "away" from sold comp 1 to make it similar to the subject property.

Total deduction -2000 + -1500= -3500 total Net adjustment.

Chapter

8

HOW TO PRICE THE HOME CORRECTLY

How to price the home correctly:

When searching for the comparables to use in your analysis remember to check the tax records for the assessed value and other characteristics.

When finding the comparables you would like to use, it is important to create a bracket of at least 10-40 grand, but no more than a 50 grand gap in pricing.

After finding three similar sold and three similar active listings that you would like to use in the bpo the task of pricing the home correctly comes into play. This is a crucial part of performing a bpo analysis.

The final price of a bpo is going to depend on the comparables that you used and the prices you obtained both before and after the adjustments were made.

The action of finding the price range to price the home with will be called bracketing.

We bracket our values to ensure that we can support the price of the home based on both our active and sold comps provided in the report. By bracketing our values, we are able to create a range that we can support the given value in our bpo with both our active and sold comps.

For example.

If I had a sold range of 120,000 to 150,000 and an active range of 130,000 – 140,000 and I wanted to give the property a final value of 120,000 that value would only be supported by my sold comps, as the lowest active value is 130,000.

If I wanted to price the home at 150,000, the actives would not support this conclusion as my highest active comp is 140,000.

However, If I priced the home anywhere from 130,000 -140,000 that would fall into both pricing ranges of my solds and actives and would be supported by both for final value conclusion.

So we bracket to find the range between our comp values that will allow both active values and sold values to be supported at the final value conclusion.

Follow these steps to find your subjects price range:

1. Take the lowest sold price and the highest sold price of the unadjusted prices – write it down
2. Take the lowest active listing price and the highest active listing price of the unadjusted prices – write it down
3. You have formed two brackets at this point, the sold bracket and the active bracket
4. Take the highest low price and the lowest high price.
5. This becomes your unadjusted bracket.

sold		Active	
$	120,000.00	$	145,900.00
$	141,000.00	$	129,500.00
$	137,900.00	$	135,000.00
sold		120,000–141,000	
active		129,500–145,900	
bracket		(129,500–141,000)	
of pricing			

6. Next you take a look at your adjusted bracket; this means the increases or decreases to the sales price of a comparable property to arrive at an indicated value for the property being appraised.
7. Again follow the procedure above with bracketing the adjusted prices, take the lowest sold price and the highest sold price and write it down.
8. Take the lowest active listing price and the highest active listing price after adjustments and write it down.
9. Again, you have a range of sold listing values and active listing values.

sold	Active
$ 133,500.00	$ 165,900.00
$ 140,000.00	$ 129,500.00
$ 129,000.00	$ 138,000.00
sold	129,000–140,000
active	129,500–165,900
bracket	(129,500–140,000)
of pricing	

10. Now that you have a bracket of both unadjusted and adjusted prices you have to bracket them one more time to find your price range for the subject property. Again take the highest lowest and the lowest highest and that is your bracket to price.

unadjusted	129,500–141,000
adjusted	129,500–140,000
bracket of pricing home	(129,500–140,000)

11. Price the home based on your opinion of condition, location, and qualities with regard to the subject versus the comparable properties, you may choose to price the home higher in the bracket, or in the middle of the bracket. If you feel the home may not sell at the highest price in the bracket, price it at the lowest amount in your bracket. Picking the exact price is up to your discretion. The fact is that when you picked the comparables, you already justified pricing the home based on the comparables in the current market.

12. Add comments regarding how you derived at the price in the bpo form for example *"value derived from both unadjusted and adjusted values of comparables, due to location and condition of property, priced home to sell within given time frame."*

13. There are generally different slots for pricing on every form, meaning there will be numerous decisions to make in the pricing section of the bpo. They often inquire if the home should be sold as is or with repairs, that is up to your discretion, but remember all repairs must be listed in the repair addendum. Also, they want a 60, 90 and 120 day pricing suggestion regarding the marketing period. The marketing time is the period of time between the start of the marketing of the home to sell and the final closing time. Let talk a little more about these pricing elements.

    a. As is – this means the home should be sold with no repairs as it is sitting on the market at the current time. This price would be the same as repaired if there were no repairs needed to the home.

    b. Repaired – This is requiring the as is price be adjusted to show all the repairs that you listed for the home. So the repaired price is the as is + repaired value. Again, if there were no repairs needed to the home, the repaired value would be the same value of the as is price.

c. *60, 90, 120* day marketing strategy – This is a field that some bpo forms sometimes have that would require you to price the home based on the timeline of marketing the home. Here are some basic tips to follow.

  o In a declining market, you would price the home highest price to lowest price suggestion. Meaning that over time, the price of the home would decline.

  o If it is a stable market, you pick one price and use it on all three marketing times.

  o If the market is increasing, you would start with a low pricing strategy and gradually increase it over the marketing time.

Take a look at this example chart which shows how to price based on the given market conditions:

Example bracket (120,000-130,000)	60 day value	90 day value	120 day value
declining market	130,000	125,000	120,000
stable market	130,000	130,000	130,000
increasing market	120,000	125,000	130,000

More Examples,

To really become a pricing Pro, it takes practice. I think it is best to see examples and practice before the BPOs start rolling in. Here are some examples to view on the following page regarding how to price a home.

Example 1:

Unadjusted Sold	Unadjusted Active		Adjusted Sold	Adjusted Active
253,000	285,000		273,000	265,000
290,000	297,000		293,000	279,000
274,500	265,500		274,500	271,000

Unadjusted Sold:	253,000-290,000	Adjusted Sold:	273,000-293,000	
Unadjusted Active:	265,500-297,000	Adjusted Active	271,000-279,000	
Unadjusted Bracket	265,500-290,000	Adjusted Bracket	273,000-279,000	
	Unadjusted	265,500-290,000		
	Adjusted	273,000-279,000		
	price home between	273,000-279,900		

Example 2:

Unadjusted Sold	Unadjusted Active	Adjusted Sold	Adjusted Active
43,000	44,900	47,000	45,900
47,925	46,900	51,200	50,900
69,900	71,000	72,500	70,000

Unadjusted Sold: 43,000–69,900   Adjusted Sold: 47,000–72,500
Unadjusted Active: 44,900–71,000   Adjusted Active: 45,900–70,000

Unadjusted Bracket 44,900–69,900   Adjusted Bracket 47,000–70,000

Unadjusted   44,900–69,900
Adjusted   47,000–70,000

price home between 47,000–69,900

Watch Out:

Sometimes when we are pricing, we make too many adjustments or don't have a large enough bracket. Here are some warnings to be aware of regarding pricing:

1. No bracket at all. Make sure you have a bracket with positive numbers. Example 120,000-130,000, if your bracket becomes 130,000-120,000 this is a negative bracket and you cannot price a home with this. Your bracket should always flow from the lowest to highest number.

2. Small bracket. When you have your bracket between adjusted and unadjusted values, and your bracket becomes very small, for example 125,500 – 125,700, there is not enough pricing leeway to price the home correctly. Look back at your adjustments and change some items to create a larger pricing bracket.

3. Huge bracket, this can sometimes be a hang up because the client request comps similar to subject, if you do have a large bracket, be sure to make adjustments so that you can narrow down the pricing and be more persuasive with your price analysis.

Remember this while bracketing:
Take the Highest Lowest and the Lowest Highest!

Steps to fill in the Pricing section:

After your bracket is formed, you can then price the home in the pricing section of the bpo form. Some forms ask for multiple pricing suggestions based on as is and repaired values and others only want one value for the home. In this example, we will view a pricing section that requires as is value, repaired value and 30 day as is value.

	Market Value	Suggested List Price
As Is	$	$
Repaired	$	$
30 As Is	$	$
Land Value	$	

Remember:

<u>As Is:</u> **This is the price the home will sell for currently on the market with no repairs**

<u>Repaired:</u> **This is the price the home will sell for currently on the market after all repairs are made. Repaired value should always be the highest**

<u>30 as-is value:</u> **Distressed value that the home would sell for in 30 days or less. This should always be the lowest value given to the property**

<u>Land value:</u> **Value of land alone (obtain from tax records)**

<u>List price:</u> **should always be higher than market value.**

In this pricing example our range of value is 109,000 – 125,000
No repairs needed

	Market Value		Suggested List Price
As Is	$ 122,000	$	125,000
Repaired	$ 122,000	$	125,000
30 As Is	$ 109,000	$	111,000
Land Value	$ 10,000		

Pricing Steps:

1. 30 AS market value (put the lowest value in your range)
2. 30 AS IS list price (add 2000-3000 K to 30 AS IS market value to obtain a list price)
3. Repaired List price (put the highest value in your range)
4. Repaired Market Value (Subtract 2000-3000 from Repaired list price to obtain a market value)
5. AS IS list Price (Repaired list price – all repairs)
6. AS IS market value (Repaired Market value – all repairs)
7. Land value obtained from tax records

Remember:

- List price should always be higher than market value and should be based on your areas statistic of list price vs sales price.
- 30 day AS IS should always be lower than both Repaired and AS IS values.
- No values should go outside pricing bracket of sold and active comps used in the report. Price using your bracket and you will always avoid going outside the sold and active values, remember, this bracket allows you to have values that will support both sold and active value ranges.
- No values should overlap

Let's look at a pricing example of a home that needs repairs:

**In this pricing example our range of value is 109,000 – 125,000.
The home needs a total of $ 8,000 of Repairs.**

	Market Value		Suggested List Price
As Is	$ 114,000	$	117,000
Repaired	$ 122,000	$	125,000
30 As Is	$ 109,000	$	111,000
Land Value	$ 10,000		

The repaired value section (market value and listing value) should always be the highest amount in the pricing section. The as is section is where you subtract repaired value- repairs to obtain the value for that section (market value and suggested list price)

In this example I took my repaired market value 122,000 and subtracted 8000 of repairs to get 114,000 as my as is market value.

Next, I took my repaired list price of 125,000 and subtracted 8,000 of repairs to get my 117,000 as is suggested list price.

We must use our good judgment as agents when pricing a home. The above is only an example to show fundamental. When we have our value range, it is up to us to apply the adjustments and take the value of the home. We do not always have to use the high range of our value, or the low range of our value to price. We may feel the home is better priced in the median value range we have created and can price from there using these fundamental pricing instructions.

9

HOW TO USE A BPO COMPARABLE TEMPLATE

How to Use a BPO Comparable Template:

When I first started doing bpos, I hand wrote all my subject, and comparable information on paper. Man did my hand hurt by the end of the day! Over time I learned Microsoft Excel is a BPO agent's best friend. Using Excel, you can create a template to store and even import all your bpo data in one place. It is simply not efficient to type what you research directly into the data entry screen for the bpo company. The BPO comparable template can be created as a cheat sheet when researching the subject property and comparables. This form allows you to do the research first and then have a great template to do your data entry from. Also, it helps for record purposes, BPO records need to be kept for a minimum of 1 year, and most recommended to keep the records for at least 5 years. Check with your local state regulations to get more information regarding the time table for holding BPO records.

This example form has room for two different bpo's. The top half of the page could be used for one bpo, while the bottom half could be used for another bpo. **A bpo requires subject property information as well as 3 sold comparables and 3 active comparables.**

The following are the fields that you will need to research and add to your comparables form:

- ✓ **MLS #**
- ✓ **Status**
- ✓ **Address**
- ✓ **zip code**
- ✓ **square footage**
- ✓ **bed**
- ✓ **bath**

- ✓ lot size
- ✓ garage
- ✓ basement
- ✓ age
- ✓ list date or sold date
- ✓ days on the market
- ✓ original list price
- ✓ current list price or sold price
- ✓ closing costs

When doing the bpo, first gather subject information. After finding all necessary information for the subject property, start locating and entering the same information for the sold and active comparables you would like to use.

Let's go over the different aspects of this form. **Please remember, most MLS systems can export this data from your MLS to excel CSV file, in which you don't even have to manually write your comps down on paper or type them into excel.**

SUBJECT: 2385 miller bottom rd

Listing #	tatu	Full Street Address	Zip	Sqft	oor/B	Datl	Al	Lot	Bar	Base	Age	Ld	Cd	Dom	Old	lp	sp	CC	Typ
		2385 miller bottom rd	30052	1600	6	3	2	0	2.80	2c	1200	1974								
3266751	Sol	3909 Grove Trl	30052	1640	8	4	2	1	.69 Ac	2	1501	1984	8/2/2012 0:00	11/16/2012 0:00	41	130000	130000	130000	0	r
7002020	Sol	355 Brand Rd	30052	1841	6	3	2	1	1.5 Ac	2	1329	1975	10/4/2012 0:00	12/5/2012 0:00	31	125000	120000	117500	3347	f
7008111	Sol	3332 Oak Grove Rd 158	30052	1520	6	3	2	0	201xx	2	1488	1968	10/19/2012 0:00	11/16/2012 0:00	25	125000	125000	125000	4859	r
7010330	Ac	3667 Tom Brewer Rd	30052	1690	6	3	2	0	2.68 Ac	2	n	1983	10/25/2012 0:00		140	142900	142900				r
7019177	Ac	3722 Oak Grove Rd	30052	1900	6	3	2	0	1.71	2	n	1977	11/16/2012 0:00		66	131580	121125				f
7001760	Ac	6030 Sandy Creek Rd	30052	1745	8	4	3	1	1.873	2	1326	1964	10/5/2012 0:00		157	149000	137000				r

	RF#	c0120000000070000	Sub.			t	1582.49	none	Notes
Sold Date	12/12/2005	land	51660	ompai	grc		none		
BPO2		price	175000	storie	1 st		Bracket: 121125-130000		
		Tax As.	139631						

no hoa

SUBJECT: 2751 ozora church rd

Listing #	tatu	Full Street Address	Zip	Sqft	oor/B	Datl	Al	Lot	Bar	Base	Age	Ld	Cd	Dom	Old	lp	sp	CC	Typ
		2751 ozora church rd	30052	2031	5	3	2	1	3.15	2	n	1988								
7019060	Sol	3204 Holly Stand Ct	30052	2305	8	4	3	1	4	2	1326	1993	11/18/2012 0:00	2/18/2013 0:00	74	179000	179000	170000	0	r
7019646	Sol	2438 Claude Brewer Rd	30052	2112	8	3	2	1	1 ACR	2	n	1997	11/19/2012 0:00	1/9/2013 0:00	29	115000	115000	115000	1200	f
7027371	Sol	3617 Malachi Way	30052	2260	8	3	3	1	1.0 Ac	2	1402	1992	12/12/2012 0:00	1/10/2013 0:00	21	169900	169900	162500	0	r
7027811	Ac	2989 Old Zion Cemetery	30052	2150	8	4	3	1	1.37	2	n	1988	12/13/2012 0:00		90	175000	139000				f
7049259	Un	5355 Forest Falls Dr	30052	2099	8	3	2	1	4	2	1390	1993	2/5/2013 0:00		12	124900	134900				f
7064188	Ne	2660 Round Ridge Rd	30052	2135	8	4	2	1	2.10	2	n	1978	3/11/2013 0:00		3	165000	165000				r

	RF#	r5197010	Sub.		3534.93	cheek estates	Notes
Sold Date	5/3/2011	Land	86600	ompai	grc	cheek estates	
		Sold $	363000	storie	1 st	Bracket: 134900-165000	
		Tax As.	213800				

no hoa

Looking at the examples:

I have designated a line for the subject property information. Then the next three rows are reserved for the sold comparables and the final three rows are reserved for the active comparables.

Is the subject property currently listed in MLS?

In both of these examples, the home is not currently listed. If the home were listed however, the template would have the following info in the subject row: List date, days on the market, original list price and current list price. Also, in the Notes box below, all listing info such as mls number, listing agent and contact info would be notated for the subject property listing.

Tax Information:

All subject property data should be thorough; with this in mind it is helpful to first look up the subject address in the tax database. The tax information should provide the following information for the subject property: RF number of Tax Id, land value estimation, annual tax estimation, tax value estimation, last sold date, subdivision name, stories and details of the subject property such as square footage, bed and bath count, lot size, year built etc.

MLS numbers:

These are sometimes required for orders and other times not required. I recommend that you read client instructions and look at the bpo form before you start researching the order. If the order requests mls numbers, make sure to record the data or export the data so that you don't have to go back to the data source a second time.

Bed Section:

The bed section that you see in the examples above has two different numbers in the square. I will explain why this is. The first number is the total room count, and then the actual bedroom count. For example, 8/4 means 8 total rooms, 4 bedrooms.

Basement:

The basement section will either have a N for No basement, or a Y for yes there is a basement; please make sure to include the square footage for the basement.

Age:

You could choose to write the year built as the examples are above or you could calculate the age of the property. It is more common for the bpo forms to require the year built than the calculated age of the property.

Current Price:

The current price section requires that you put the current price for the active listings and the sold price for the sold listings.

Notes Section:

Some homes have annual association fees, which need to be noted for the bpo. Feel free to put the information into the notes section of the bpo form. You could also add amenities included such as swim or tennis.

Left side of form:

You can use the free space out to the left of the home to write anything regarding particular comparables, maybe you could write the type of sale for example resale or REO. Other examples could include newly renovated comments, fixer upper etc. Sometimes when the sold comps are selling for more than what the list price was it was overbidding that occurred. This is a great space to write overbidding so that you remember to make comments regarding this in the bpo section.

Pricing:

Numbers written to the left side of the paper toward the bottom of the bpo sections are the pricing brackets. This section will allow you to write your range of pricing for the bpo.

Create an Export template straight out of MLS.

You must check with your local MLS to see if this is possible before considering this as your option for pulling subject data. Most MLS will allow you to create a template and save it in your MLS system. You can then search your comps and export them out in your saved template format.

If you decide to take this route, it is handy to have your subject tax record printed out and in front of you while doing your data entry into the BPO.

Use the following fields to create an export template:

- ✓ MLS #
- ✓ Status
- ✓ Address

- ✓ City
- ✓ zip code
- ✓ square footage
- ✓ bed
- ✓ bath
- ✓ lot size
- ✓ garage
- ✓ basement
- ✓ basement square footage
- ✓ age
- ✓ list date
- ✓ sold date
- ✓ days on the market
- ✓ original list price
- ✓ current list price
- ✓ sold price
- ✓ closing costs

Chapter

10

HOW TO ADDRESS
A KICKBACK

How to Address a Kickback:

What is a kickback:

A kickback or clarification request is when the QC department finds an error or discrepancy with the bpo your submitted. This can be caused by many things, such as uploaded the wrong photos, and didn't bracket the home price between sold values, difference in value between previous report and current report. The list goes on and on.

Here are some pointers to addressing kickbacks.

- Before submitting the order, make sure to look over the bpos to look for errors.
- Respond to the kickback and resubmit the order as soon as possible.
- Read the clarification request comments from the QC department and truly understand what they are saying needs correcting or adjusting.
- Go back through your order making the corrections needed from the qc department.
- Most orders have a way you can validate them to see if any errors pop up.

Difference in Value between past and current reports:

This means that there was a previous report on file that had a significantly different value for the subject property. Does this mean you priced in incorrectly? No. This means that you have to be able to defend why you priced the home at that value. They usually send you comps that were used in a prior report so that you can see if these comps were more similar to the subject than the comps you used. Take the time to look up each comp, look at their amenities, construction, lot size and square footage. In other words, go through the MLS page with a fine tooth comb and find a reason why the home is not as similar as the comparables you used.

If you look through the suggested comps and realize they are better comps for the subject property, consider changing your price of the subject property and changing comps you used in the report. This kickback can be time consuming, but you owe it to your customers to give them the product they expect. If you feel you overpriced it originally, swallow your pride and make the correction.

Learn from the Kickback:

Clarification requests often hurt your overall quality score, so you want to minimize the amount of kickbacks you get. It is important to learn from every kickback and take something from it as a lesson to do on your next order. Maybe next time you will double check this or that. Take it as a learning experience and try not to get frustrated.

11

TAKING THE
PHOTOS

Taking the Photos:

This can sometimes be an exciting part of the job, other times... *(Like when you're caught taking a photo of a home, and the homeowner yells out, Hey what are you doing?!?!?!)*.......a little awkward.

When doing an exterior bpo on a home, the directions within the solicitation require that you not trespass onto the property, and not to speak with any home owners regarding what you're doing. Here are some general requirements to consider regarding bpo photos:

Photo requirements:

- Time and date stamp on the photos
- Check within each individual order to see what photos they need you to take. For example on company may want a front view, street view and address verification. Another company may want two street views, two side views, one front view and one street view plus an address verification photo. It is imperative that you know what the photo requirements are before going out to take the photo.
- Do not trespass
- Do not get photos of the car you're driving in or any part of your body in the picture. These pictures need to look professional. Envision this as your listing and you are going to put these photos on MLS.
- YOU the licensed agent must be the one taking the photos do not try to outsource this job to someone else. These companies are paying you to do it with the impression that you are going out to the home to inspect the home yourself.
- Interior bpo orders require a photo of every room, also make sure to take photos of the ac unit, water heater and breaker

box as well. Not all companies require this, but it is safe to go the extra mile and get all the photos while you are in the home.

General Photo Requirements

<u>**Exterior orders–**</u>

- ✓ Front
- ✓ 2 sides (right and left)
- ✓ street view
- ✓ address verification photo
- ✓ garage

<u>**Interior orders-**</u>

- ✓ Front
- ✓ 2 sides (right and left)
- ✓ back view
- ✓ street view
- ✓ address verification photo
- ✓ garage
- ✓ repairs
- ✓ 1 photo of every interior room of the home

Be sure to read the client instructions for every bpo you get to determine if they require more photos to be taken than those listed above. Some bpo companies do ask for photos of what the home faces, as well as other shots, so make sure that you know what they want before you set off to take the photos.

Address verification photos are very important; however sometimes when you go to a home, there is no numbered address on the property. If this occurs, its best practice to take a photo of a neighboring property address and the street sign. You can notate the report that the subject property had not physical address present, that neighboring address photo was uploaded in order to show address verification of subject.

Repairs:

Interior and exterior BPO's require you to list all repairs visible to the eye when completing the report. When you are out at the home photographing the property, you need to take photos of the repairs as well. It is handy when completing multiple BPO's in a day to create a repair template for each interior home you visit.

The repair template example on the next page is a great place to start. You simply list the address on the template and check by any boxes that show the needed repairs of the home. I have a laminated copy of this template. When I go to the home, I write on my laminated copy with a dry erase marker and then take a picture of the template to have with my subject photos. I then erase the template and move on to the next home.

Before you start doing BPO's, it's imperative to check repair costs in your area. Repairs can vary in cost by region. Make sure your repair estimates meet or exceeds the Federal Housing Administration and HUD compliance guidelines for local repair cost estimates.

Repair type	Amount	Required
Trash Out		
Initial Clean		
mailbox missing		
pressure wash exterior		
Yard Maintenance / Cut		
Replace Carpet		
refinish hardwood floor		
Interior Paint		
replace kitchen cabinents		
replace kitchen countertop		
replace linoleum		
toliet missing		
bathroom mirrors		
missing sink		
bathroom cabinents missing		
missing fridge		
missing stove		
missing dishwasher		
missing washer/dryer		
broken window (s)		
replace door (s)		
repair drywall		
replace deck		
exterior paint		
new roof		
replace garage door		
trim/ cut trees		
missing ac unit		
missing hot water heater		

NOTES:

12

CREATING AN EFFECTIVE ROUTE

Creating an efficient Route:

To be successful within the bpo industry, you have to have a game plan. For example, I only go take photos three times a week. This means that I have to rely on efficient routing to get all the photos needed into my route for each particular day. I have mentioned before that a GPS system is priceless in this industry, but you have to go a step further to become an efficient router. This skill can save you hours of your time daily!

You have to decide a time of day that you will be taking your photos. I must hint that it is not the best time of day to go in early morning or afternoon traffic, so plan accordingly. After you have picked a time to run your daily route, you need to pick a cut off time for adding photos to the route. What I mean by this is that sometimes you have to go to multiple cities or areas that are a good distance away from each other. If you accept an order and have already passed that area in your route, it doesn't make since to turn around and go back and take the other photo. This kills your time and your plan for the rest of the day. Put the new order on the next route and continue with the route you are running.

An efficient route should be from your office to all your stops and back to your office creating a circular or tear drop shape on a map. I recommend you type or import all your addresses into a routing system. Put the homes in the order that you think would make a good map and then see what kind of shape comes up. Here is a hint, Keep moving forward, no backtracking.

Although this may seem minuscule in connection with all the other assignments to complete a bpo, this is a time saving technique that should be implemented for your success.

More Tips on Creating an efficient Route:

This is a production based job, so the quicker you go, the more you make. Creating an efficient route will help you make the most money in the least amount of time. It is crucial to use routing software to get all the photos needed into your route for each particular day.

Print out a list for the road:

You need to have a printed list of all addresses you will be visiting. This will help you keep up with your stops and also help you visualize your progress when you are out driving. I recommend using excel to list out all your addresses. You can print this page, import it into mapping systems and also save it for your records.

Steps to route:

- ✓ Compile your bpo excel list of stops
- ✓ Print out a copy of your stops
- ✓ Decide the order of your route based on your cities assigned.
- ✓ Import or copy/paste addresses into the routing system
- ✓ After you have entered or uploaded all stops, drag the addresses to put them in the most efficient order, you should see the map to the right begin to make a circle.
- ✓ As you have put all the addresses in order for that city, number your stops on your excel print out.
- ✓ At the end of the process, you should have all stops numbered on your excel print out and you are ready to drive.

13

METHODS TO TRACK
YOUR BPO WORK

Methods to Track you BPO work:

The idea behind becoming a very profitable BPO vendor is to have as many companies as possible sending you work. Because you will have different companies it is necessary to track your work.

Tracking your work will help you in the following ways:

- Tax time
- Monthly calculation of earnings
- Tracking progress and exact number of bpo's done monthly
- Tracking pay schedules
- Identifies what companies are providing you with the most work

I recommend that you use Excel to track your work on a monthly basis. Set up an excel workbook that you could use for the entire year. Make sure the workbook is broken down by month, and automatically calculates earned money on a monthly basis. It has fields that require the address, company that assigned the order, amount of money for the order and date completed.

address	company	amount	date	completed
2505 RICHARDS WALK LOGANVILLE GA 30052	PROTK	$ 40.00	5/2/2013	
209 RAVENWOOD CT BETHELEHEM GA 30620	PROTK	$ 10.00	5/1/2013	
6594 N HIGHWAY 81 LOGANVILLE GA 30052	CLEAR CAPITAL	$ 40.00	5/2/2013	
715 CAYLA ANN CT. LOGANVILLE GA 30052	CLEAR CAPITAL	$ 40.00	5/2/2013	
1037 richmond place way loganville ga 30052	CLEAR CAPITAL	$ 55.00	5/2/2013	
6495 old mill ln. monroe ga 30655	CLEAR CAPITAL	$ 55.00	5/2/2013	
660 herring rd. grayson ga 30017	CLEAR CAPITAL	$ 55.00	5/2/2013	
959 nestling dr. lawenville ga 30045	CLEAR CAPITAL	$ 55.00	5/2/2013	
249 stargrass way grayson ga 30017	CLEAR CAPITAL	$ 55.00	5/2/2013	
1033 richmond place way loganville ga 30052	CLEAR CAPITAL	$ 55.00	5/2/2013	
715 windsor brook ln. lawrenceville ga 30045	protk	$ 40.00	5/2/2013	
2618 britt trail dr. lawrenceville ga 30045	CLEAR CAPITAL	$ 55.00	5/2/2013	
432 grassmeade way snellville ga 30078	CLEAR CAPITAL	$ 10.00	5/2/2013	
863 windwward rd. winder ga 30680	protk	$ 40.00	5/3/2013	
1110 mcree mill ln. watkinsville ga 30677	CLEAR CAPITAL	$ 40.00	5/3/2013	
635 willowwind dr. loganville ga 30052	CLEAR CAPITAL	$ 40.00	5/6/2013	
3715 LINWOOD WAY SNELLVILLE GA 30039	GREEN RIVER CAPITAL	$ 72.50	5/5/2013	3706
2149 OAKRIDGE AVE MONROE GA 30656	GREEN RIVER CAPITAL	$ 72.50	5/5/2013	2106
2149 OAKRIDGE AVE MONROE GA 30656	GREEN RIVER CAPITAL	$ 17.50	5/5/2013	2106
2405 BOONE CT. SNELLVILLE GA 30078	GREEN RIVER CAPITAL	$ 72.50	5/5/2013	2406
3297 PATE CREEK VIEW SNELLVILLE GA 30078	GREEN RIVER CAPITAL	$ 47.50	5/5/2013	2406

week 1   52 orders   2617.5
7 protk
22 clear capital
21 green river cap
2 valuation vision

week 2   58 orders   2722.5
39 green river capital
1 blue mtn.
1 protk
7 clear capital
10 mainstreet

week 3   50 ord
43 green river cap
1 protk
6 clear capital

week 4   5 orde
2 clear capital
3 green river capi

Sheet tabs: January, February, March, April, May, June, July, August, September, October, November, December

Instructions for Creating a BPO Tracking Excel Workbook

One tool that is great for tracking your bpo work is Excel. I have provided an example template for you that shows you how you can track and tally monthly the income your are bringing in from your bpo business. Let's go over each field of the workbook so that you can use it to its potential.

Address: This is where you should put the property address of the bpo assigned, be sure to put the entire address for your tracking advantage.

Company: Put the company name that assigned you the order, this will help because you will be able to search how many you did for a specific company or simply be able to track their individual payments.

Payment: Keep track of what they are paying you to do the order, every company is different, so you must fill in the correct amount paid for the work done. The excel workbook can be modified to automatically add all the figures you put into the payment section, so you don't have to do the adding, excel will take care of that for you.

Date: Put the date you completed the order, this will help with tracking purposes. Some companies have dates of cutoff for payments on orders, when you put the date you submitted it to the company this will sometimes help you track when you get paid.

Add columns: Feel free to add any columns you would think will help you track your orders better, some put the order number as a column for tracking purposes, others may want to put a date assigned column to add to your complete date and track your turn around time.

Add rows: You will have to add rows when you start getting more bpos. To do this, highlight some rows in the spreadsheet and right click, then select "insert." If you do this in the area that is already made as the spreadsheet it will keep the sum formula that is put into excel, so your numbers will continue to add properly.

SAVE, SAVE, SAVE: It is very important that you save the excel workbook every time you enter something into it. You do not want to lose this data. Get into a habit of hitting save every time you exit out of the workbook, even if you didn't make any additions or changes to the information.

Chapter

GETTING PAID

14

Getting Paid:

You have to check with your broker to see the procedure of getting paid from BPO providers. Some brokers require the check to be made out to the firm and then they cut you another check. Other Brokers allow the check to be mailed straight to you.

It is recommended that when checks come in you log the date, company that sent them and the amount of the checks for your record. One way to do this is to get a receipt book from an office supply store. This will help you track your income for tax time.

Make sure to highlight the orders that you were paid for on your excel tracking template to ensure all of your work gets paid for and nothing is left out.

Make sure that every company that you get solicitations from have an updated W-9 on file for you, as sometimes this can delay payments.

Every bpo company is different in the way that they cut the checks. Some companies cut the checks every thirty days, others cut the checks every sixty days, and some cut checks two times a month. You will have to check with each company to determine what their pay schedule is and then you will need to plan accordingly.

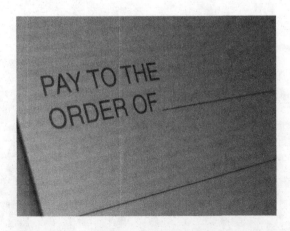

15

USE BPO EXPERIENCE TO FURTHER YOUR CAREER

Use your BPO Experience to Catapult your career to the next level

The best thing about becoming a successful BPO agent is all of the experience you gain while performing your bpos. You can use your bpo knowledge for multiple angles in the real estate market to advance yourself and your career. Let's look at some of the ways becoming a bpo expert can help you out.

Market Expert:

When you say Market Expert, you think of an agent that has their finger on the pulse of the neighborhood. Examine new listings, reviewing sold comps, being knowledgeable about schools, market statistics and overall pace of the neighborhood. By preforming BPOs in your area, you are practicing and molding these skills. You will begin to memorize market activity within your area and have strong knowledge of your community. You will be able to stay abreast with all local trends, because you are already researching the area with every BPO you perform. When you are assisting buyers in the area, use this market knowledge and show them you are a market expert.

Listing appointments:

One of the hardest things when I first started real estate was learning truly how to price a home. Sure we learn about CMAs in real estate school, then we are taught how to pull them in our real estate systems but its not a truly accurate number until you learn to do adjustments to value for the comparable. BPOs allow you to become a CMA pro. Not only pulling comps similar to the home you want to list, but to be able to apply adjustments and create a pricing range will allow you to not only look like a real estate professional to the seller, but will guarantee your listings will not sit on the market due to being overpriced. We know that pricing the home is the most important step to selling the home. Be an expert by practicing with each BPO you perform. This will give you confidence and know how to approach sellers with accurate information.

Lets talk about how you can use this same BPO knowledge to inform the seller why they should go with you over the other agents they may interview for the job of selling their home. What's my angle? Well, you are a pricing expert, the fact that you work for many asset companies preforming price analysis on many homes in the community makes you one. Use this fact to plug into any listing presentation this will help build credibility and respect with your sellers.

Investor relationships:

A talent I formed while doing bpos is the ability to see potential investment opportunities for investors. Over time, you develop the ability to see homes that would make great rental properties, or great flips. You are combing your MLS looking for comps for this bpo, but at the same time discovering diamond in the ruff properties that are waiting for an investor buyer to find them and rehab them. Use this to your advantage, search online and find investors, once you find a great flip property submit the information to them. I closed 21 deals this year based off of this one principle I like to call scrubbing. If a home is underpriced in a market of homes showing significantly higher market value that's a great start for a potential investor deal. Dig into it and see if your research will have you writing contracts too!

16

FUNDAMENTAL
BPO CONCEPTS
WORKBOOK

Adjustments Practice: *Use the following sample to practice your adjustments.*

- Seller concessions (– exact amount)
- Bedrooms (+ or – 2000)
- Bathrooms (+ or – 1500)
- Basements (+ or – 10000)
- Lot size (+ or – 2000 per acre)
- Garage (+ or – 1000)
- Age (+ or – 5000) for properties older than or newer than 10 years of subject.
- Sq ft (+ or – 1000) per 100 sq ft extra

characteristics	Subject property	comparable 1	adjustment	comparable 2	adjustment	comparable 3	adjustment
sq footage	3006	2980		2890		3126	
year built	2006	1995		2002		2008	
lot size	1 acre	2 acres		3 acres		5 acres	
bedrooms	4	3		4		2	
bathrooms	3	1		3		2	
total							

characteristics	Subject property	comparable 1	adjustment	comparable 2	adjustment	comparable 3	adjustment
sq footage	2180	2260		2450		1980	
year built	1985	1975		1980		1970	
lot size	0.36 acres	0.56 acres		0.4 acres		0.26 acres	
bedrooms	5	4		3		5	
bathrooms	3	3		2		4	
total							

characteristics	Subject property	comparable 1	adjustment	comparable 2	adjustment	comparable 3	adjustment
sq footage	1590	2060		1499		1309	
year built	1980	1995		1990		1988	
garage	2 car	1 car		2 car		3 car	
bedrooms	5	3		4		6	
bathrooms	2	2		3		3	
total							

characteristics	Subject property	comparable 1	adjustment	comparable 2	adjustment	comparable 3	adjustment
concessions	0	1590		4000			
year built	2014	2000		2005			
lot size	6 acres	3 acres		10 acres			
bedrooms	3	5		4			
Basement	0	920		1523			
total							

Bracketing Practice:

Find the pricing bracket for the following example pricing problems. Remember to watch out for no brackets, small brackets or brackets with too large value range. Mark them with their specific problem if you come across one with a bracketing problem.

Sold Values:	Active Values:	
166,700	169,000	S: _____ _____
154,900	171,000	A: _____ _____
136,500	150,000	
		Price Bracket: _____ _____

Sold Values:	Active Values:	
69,000	73,000	S: _____ _____
72,400	71,000	A: _____ _____
52,000	79,000	
		Price Bracket: _____ _____

Sold Values:	Active Values:	
204,900	205,000	S: _____ _____
202,000	210,000	A: _____ _____
199,900	215,000	
		Price Bracket: _____ _____

Sold Values:	Active Values:	S:	_____	_____
194,000	199,900			
310,000	207,000	A:	_____	_____
188,000	299,000			
		Price Bracket:	_____	_____

Sold Values:	Active Values:	S:	_____	_____
133,000	110,000			
115,000	142,000	A:	_____	_____
127,000	129,000			
		Price Bracket:	_____	_____

Sold Values:	Active Values:	S:	_____	_____
149,900	148,000			
150,000	136,000	A:	_____	_____
153,000	155,000			
		Price Bracket:	_____	_____

Sold Values:	Active Values:	S:	_____	_____
36,000	32,000			
47,000	49,000	A:	_____	_____
60,000	60,000			
		Price Bracket:	_____	_____

Sold Values:	Active Values:	S:	_____	_____
174,000	155,000			
189,000	149,000	A:	_____	_____
162,000	176,000			
		Price Bracket:	_____	_____

Sold Values:	Active Values:	S:	_____	_____
122,900	119,000			
125,000	123,000	A:	_____	_____
131,000	120,000			
		Price Bracket:	_____	_____

Sold Values:	Active Values:	S:	_____	_____
326,000	331,000			
340,000	350,000	A:	_____	_____
332,000	345,000			
		Price Bracket:	_____	_____

Sold Values:	Active Values:	S:	_____	_____
15,000	16,000			
65,000	79,000	A:	_____	_____
75,900	46,000			
		Price Bracket:	_____	_____

Adjusted vs unadjusted bracketing practice:

Take the adjusted value and unadjusted values to form a final pricing bracket.

Unadjusted Range:	136000	175000
Adjusted Range:	129000	160000
Final Pricing Bracket:	_____	_____
Unadjusted Range:	56000	80000
Adjusted Range:	56000	69000
Final Pricing Bracket:	_____	_____
Unadjusted Range:	198000	212000
Adjusted Range:	196000	209000
Final Pricing Bracket:	_____	_____
Unadjusted Range:	145000	160000
Adjusted Range:	142000	163000
Final Pricing Bracket:	_____	_____
Unadjusted Range:	150000	169000
Adjusted Range:	145000	175000
Final Pricing Bracket:	_____	_____

Unadjusted Range:	30000	60000
Adjusted Range:	31500	62900
Final Pricing Bracket:	_____	_____
Unadjusted Range:	369000	400000
Adjusted Range:	378000	390000
Final Pricing Bracket:	_____	_____
Unadjusted Range:	125000	129700
Adjusted Range:	119000	145000
Final Pricing Bracket:	_____	_____

Acres to Sq Footage Conversion Chart

Acres	Sq Footage	Acres	Sq Footage	Acres	Sq Footage	Acres	Sq Footage	Acres	Sq Footage
0.01	436	0.45	19602	0.89	38768	1.33	57935	1.77	77101
0.02	871	0.46	20038	0.9	39204	1.34	58370	1.78	77537
0.03	1307	0.47	20473	0.91	39640	1.35	58806	1.79	77972
0.04	1742	0.48	20909	0.92	40075	1.36	59242	1.8	78408
0.05	2178	0.49	21344	0.93	40511	1.37	59677	1.81	78844
0.06	2614	0.5	21780	0.94	40946	1.38	60113	1.82	79279
0.07	3049	0.51	22216	0.95	41382	1.39	60548	1.83	79715
0.08	3485	0.52	22651	0.96	41818	1.4	60984	1.84	80150
0.09	3920	0.53	23087	0.97	42253	1.41	61420	1.85	80586
0.1	4356	0.54	23522	0.98	42689	1.42	61855	1.86	81022
0.11	4792	0.55	23958	0.99	43124	1.43	62291	1.87	81457
0.12	5227	0.56	24394	1	43560	1.44	62726	1.88	81893
0.13	5663	0.57	24829	1.01	43996	1.45	63162	1.89	82328
0.14	6098	0.58	25265	1.02	44431	1.46	63598	1.9	82764
0.15	6534	0.59	25700	1.03	44867	1.47	64033	1.91	83200
0.16	6970	0.6	26136	1.04	45302	1.48	64469	1.92	83635
0.17	7405	0.61	26572	1.05	45738	1.49	64904	1.93	84071
0.18	7841	0.62	27007	1.06	46174	1.5	65340	1.94	84506
0.19	8276	0.63	27443	1.07	46609	1.51	65776	1.95	84942
0.2	8712	0.64	27878	1.08	47045	1.52	66211	1.96	85378
0.21	9148	0.65	28314	1.09	47480	1.53	66647	1.97	85813
0.22	9583	0.66	28750	1.1	47916	1.54	67082	1.98	86249
0.23	10019	0.67	29185	1.11	48352	1.55	67518	1.99	86684
0.24	10454	0.68	29621	1.12	48787	1.56	67954	2	87120
0.25	10890	0.69	30056	1.13	49223	1.57	68389		
0.26	11326	0.7	30492	1.14	49658	1.58	68825		
0.27	11761	0.71	30928	1.15	50094	1.59	69260		
0.28	12197	0.72	31363	1.16	50530	1.6	69696		
0.29	12632	0.73	31799	1.17	50965	1.61	70132		
0.3	13068	0.74	32234	1.18	51401	1.62	70567		
0.31	13504	0.75	32670	1.19	51836	1.63	71003		
0.32	13939	0.76	33106	1.2	52272	1.64	71438		
0.33	14375	0.77	33541	1.21	52708	1.65	71874		
0.34	14810	0.78	33977	1.22	53143	1.66	72310		
0.35	15246	0.79	34412	1.23	53579	1.67	72745		
0.36	15682	0.8	34848	1.24	54014	1.68	73181		
0.37	16117	0.81	35284	1.25	54450	1.69	73616		
0.38	16553	0.82	35719	1.26	54886	1.7	74052		
0.39	16988	0.83	36155	1.27	55321	1.71	74488		
0.4	17424	0.84	36590	1.28	55757	1.72	74923		
0.41	17860	0.85	37026	1.29	56192	1.73	75359		
0.42	18295	0.86	37462	1.3	56628	1.74	75794		
0.43	18731	0.87	37897	1.31	57064	1.75	76230		
0.44	19166	0.88	38333	1.32	57499	1.76	76666		

Acres to Sq ft Conversion Practice:

Use the acres to sq ft conversion chart to covert the follow site sizes. Different bpo companies can use either site measurement, so you must be prepared to convert your data, 1 acre = 43560 sq ft. So you can also take your data and multiply by sq ft or divide by lot size to get your conversion.

example: .49 acres $\star$43560 = 21344 sq ft

21344 / 43560 = .49 acres

Convert:

.51 acres	=	_____	sq ft
1.01 acres	=	_____	sq ft
.63 acres	=	_____	sq ft
44867 sq ft	=	_____	acres
19602 sq ft	=	_____	acres
.71 acres	=	_____	sq ft
.27 acres	=	_____	sq ft
1.99 acres	=	_____	sq ft
70132 sq ft	=	_____	acres
67954 sq ft	=	_____	acres
.76 acres	=	_____	sq ft
54014 sq ft	=	_____	acres
2.03 acres	=	_____	sq ft

Pricing Practice:

Use the following examples to price homes within your value range.
Please take into account repairs needed to the home. Land value will
be supplied as you would pull that info from the tax record.

Value Range: $ 100000 – 150000
Land Value: $ 30,000
Repairs: $ 4,000

	Market Value	Suggested list price
AS IS:		
REPAIRED:		
30 AS IS VALUE:		
LAND VALUE:		

Value Range: $ 112000 – 135000
Land Value: $ 25,000
Repairs: $ 2,000

	Market Value	Suggested list price
AS IS:		
REPAIRED:		
30 AS IS VALUE:		
LAND VALUE:		

Value Range: $ 135000 – 155000
Land Value: $ 15,000
Repairs: 0

	Market Value	Suggested list price
AS IS:		
REPAIRED:		
30 AS IS VALUE:		
LAND VALUE:		

Value Range: $ 59000 – 79000
Land Value: $ 5,000
Repairs: $ 1,000

	Market Value	Suggested list price
AS IS:		
REPAIRED:		
30 AS IS VALUE:		
LAND VALUE:		

Value Range: $ 311000 – 340000
Land Value: $ 65,000
Repairs: $ 12,000

	Market Value	Suggested list price
AS IS:		
REPAIRED:		
30 AS IS VALUE:		
LAND VALUE:		

Value Range: $ 123000 – 150000
Land Value: $ 25,000
Repairs: $ 2,000

	Market Value	Suggested list price
AS IS:		
REPAIRED:		
30 AS IS VALUE:		
LAND VALUE:		

Value Range: $ 136000 - 150000
Land Value: $ 24,000
Repairs: $ 0

	Market Value	Suggested list price
AS IS:		
REPAIRED:		
30 AS IS VALUE:		
LAND VALUE:		

Value Range: $ 121000 - 159000
Land Value: $ 25,000
Repairs: $ 5,000

	Market Value	Suggested list price
AS IS:		
REPAIRED:		
30 AS IS VALUE:		
LAND VALUE:		

Value Range: $ 181000 - 183000
Land Value: $ 25,000
Repairs: $ 100

	Market Value	Suggested list price
AS IS:		
REPAIRED:		
30 AS IS VALUE:		
LAND VALUE:		

Value Range:	$ 129000 - 140000
Land Value:	$ 31,000
Repairs:	$ 5,900

	Market Value	Suggested list price
AS IS:		
REPAIRED:		
30 AS IS VALUE:		
LAND VALUE:		

Value Range:	$ 63000 - 101000
Land Value:	$ 15,000
Repairs:	$ 21,500

	Market Value	Suggested list price
AS IS:		
REPAIRED:		
30 AS IS VALUE:		
LAND VALUE:		

Value Range:	$ 115000 - 121000
Land Value:	$ 20,000
Repairs:	$ 1,000

	Market Value	Suggested list price
AS IS:		
REPAIRED:		
30 AS IS VALUE:		
LAND VALUE:		

Value Range: $ 99000 - 107000
Land Value: $ 15,000
Repairs: $ 900

	Market Value	Suggested list price
AS IS:		
REPAIRED:		
30 AS IS VALUE:		
LAND VALUE:		

17

FUNDAMENTAL BPO CONCEPTS

Adjustments Answer Key:

- Seller concessions (– exact amount)
- Bedrooms (+ or – 2000)
- Bathrooms (+ or – 1500)
- Basements (+ or – 10000)
- Lot size (+ or – 2000 per acre)
- Garage (+ or – 1000)
- Age (+ or – 5000) for properties older than or newer than 10 years of subject.
- Sq ft (+ or – 1000) per 100 sq ft extra

characteristics	Subject property	comparable 1	adjustment	comparable 2	adjustment	comparable 3	adjustment
sq footage	3006	2980	1000	2890	2000	3126	-1000
year built	2006	1995	5000	2002	0	2008	0
lot size	1 acre	2 acres	-2000	3 acres	-4000	5 acres	-8000
bedrooms	4	3	-2000	4	0	2	4000
bathrooms	3	1	3000	3	0	2	1500
total			5000		-2000		-3500

characteristics	Subject property	comparable 1	adjustment	comparable 2	adjustment	comparable 3	adjustment
sq footage	2180	2260	-1000	2450	-3000	1980	2000
year built	1985	1975	0	1980	0	1970	5000
lot size	0.36 acres	0.56 acres	0	0.4 acres	0	0.26 acres	0
bedrooms	5	4	2000	3	4000	5	0
bathrooms	3	3	0	2	1500	4	-1500
total			1000		2500		5500

characteristics	Subject property	comparable 1	adjustment	comparable 2	adjustment	comparable 3	adjustment
sq footage	1590	2060	-5000	1499	1000	1309	2000
year built	1980	1995	-5000	1990	0	1988	0
garage	2 car	1 car	1000	2 car	0	3 car	-1000
bedrooms	5	3	4000	4	2000	6	-2000
bathrooms	2	2	0	3	-1500	3	-1500
total			-4000		1500		-2500

characteristics	Subject property	comparable 1	adjustment	comparable 2	adjustment	comparable 3	adjustment
concessions	0	1590	-1590	4000	-4000		0
year built	2014	2000	5000	2005	0		0
lot size	6 acres	3 acres	6000	10 acres	-8000		2000
bedrooms	3	5	-4000	4	-2000		2000
Basement	0	920	-10000	1523	-10000		0
total			-2410		-24000		4000

Bracketing Answer Key:

Sold Values:	Active Values:	S:	136500	166700
166,700	169,000			
154,900	171,000	A:	150000	171000
136,500	150,000			
		Price Bracket:	150000	166700

Sold Values:	Active Values:	S:	52000	72400
69,000	73,000			
72,400	71,000	A:	71000	79000
52,000	79,000			
SMALL BRACKET		Price Bracket:	71000	72400

Sold Values:	Active Values:	S:	199900	204900
204,900	205,000			
202,000	210,000	A:	205000	215000
199,900	215,000			
NO BRACKET !!!		Price Bracket:	205000	204900

Sold Values:	Active Values:	S:	188000	310000
194,000	199,900			
310,000	207,000	A:	199000	299000
188,000	299,000			
BRACKET TOO LARGE !!		Price Bracket:	199000	299000

Sold Values:	Active Values:	S:	115000	133000
133,000	110,000			
115,000	142,000	A:	110000	142000
127,000	129,000			
		Price Bracket:	115000	133000

Sold Values:	Active Values:	S:	149900	153000
149,900	148,000			
150,000	136,000	A:	136000	155000
153,000	155,000			
BRACKET TOO SMALL!!		Price Bracket:	149900	153000

Sold Values:	Active Values:	S:	36000	60000
36,000	32,000			
47,000	49,000	A:	32000	60000
60,000	60,000			
		Price Bracket:	36000	60000

Sold Values:	Active Values:	S:	162000	189000
174,000	155,000			
189,000	149,000	A:	149000	176000
162,000	176,000			
		Price Bracket:	162000	176000

Sold Values:	Active Values:	S:	122900	131000
122,900	119,000			
125,000	123,000	A:	119000	123000
131,000	120,000			

BRACKET TOO SMALL!!

Price Bracket: 122900   123000

Sold Values:	Active Values:	S:	326000	340000
326,000	331,000			
340,000	350,000	A:	331000	350000
332,000	345,000			

Price Bracket: 331000   340000

Sold Values:	Active Values:	S:	15000	75900
15,000	16,000			
65,000	79,000	A:	16000	79000
75,900	46,000			

BRACKET TOO BIG!!

Price Bracket: 16000   75900

Adjusted vs unadjusted Bracketing Answer Key:

Unadjusted Range:	136000	175000
Adjusted Range:	129000	160000
Final Pricing Bracket:	136000	160000

Unadjusted Range:	56000	80000
Adjusted Range:	56000	69000
Final Pricing Bracket:	56000	69000

Unadjusted Range:	198000	212000
Adjusted Range:	196000	209000
Final Pricing Bracket:	198000	209000

Unadjusted Range:	145000	160000
Adjusted Range:	142000	163000
Final Pricing Bracket:	145000	160000

Unadjusted Range:	150000	169000
Adjusted Range:	145000	175000
Final Pricing Bracket:	150000	169000

Unadjusted Range:	30000	60000
Adjusted Range:	31500	62900
Final Pricing Bracket:	31500	60000

Unadjusted Range:	369000	400000
Adjusted Range:	378000	390000
Final Pricing Bracket:	378000	390000
Unadjusted Range:	125000	129700
Adjusted Range:	119000	145000
Final Pricing Bracket:	125000	129700

Acres to Sq ft Conversion Practice:

Convert:

.51 acres	=	22216	sq ft
1.01 acres	=	43996	sq ft
.63 acres	=	27443	sq ft
44867 sq ft	=	1.03	acres
19602 sq ft	=	0.45	acres
.71 acres	=	30928	sq ft
.27 acres	=	11761	sq ft
1.99 acres	=	86684	sq ft
70132 sq ft	=	1.61	acres
67954 sq ft	=	1.56	acres
.76 acres	=	33106	sq ft
54014 sq ft	=	1.24	acres
2.03 acres	=	88426	sq ft

Pricing answer key:

Value Range: $ 100000 – 150000
Land Value: $ 30,000
Repairs: $ 4,000

	Market Value	Suggested list price
AS IS:	$ 144,000	$ 146,000
REPAIRED:	$ 148,000	$ 150,000
30 AS IS VALUE:	$ 100,000	$ 103,000
LAND VALUE:	$ 30,000	

Value Range: $ 112000 – 135000
Land Value: $ 25,000
Repairs: $ 2,000

	Market Value	Suggested list price
AS IS:	$ 132,000	$ 133,000
REPAIRED:	$ 134,000	$ 135,000
30 AS IS VALUE:	$ 112,000	$ 115,000
LAND VALUE:	$ 25,000	

Value Range: $ 135000 – 155000
Land Value: $ 15,000
Repairs: $ 0

	Market Value	Suggested list price
AS IS:	$ 153,000	$ 155,000
REPAIRED:	$ 153,000	$ 155,000
30 AS IS VALUE:	$ 135,000	$ 137,000
LAND VALUE:	$ 15,000	

Value Range: $ 59000 – 79000

Land Value: $ 5,000

Repairs: $ 1,000

	Market Value	Suggested list price
AS IS:	$ 76,000	$ 78,000
REPAIRED:	$ 77,000	$ 79,000
30 AS IS VALUE:	$ 59,000	$ 61,000
LAND VALUE:	$ 5,000	

Value Range: $ 311000 – 340000

Land Value: $ 65,000

Repairs: $ 12,000

	Market Value	Suggested list price
AS IS:	$ 326,000	$ 328,000
REPAIRED:	$ 338,000	$ 340,000
30 AS IS VALUE:	$ 311,000	$ 313,000
LAND VALUE:	$ 65,000	

Value Range: $ 123000 – 150000

Land Value: $ 25,000

Repairs: $ 2,000

	Market Value	Suggested list price
AS IS:	$ 147,000	$ 148,000
REPAIRED:	$ 149,000	$ 150,000
30 AS IS VALUE:	$ 123,000	$ 125,000
LAND VALUE:	$ 25,000	

Value Range: $ 136000 – 150000
Land Value: $ 24,000
Repairs: 0

	Market Value	Suggested list price
AS IS:	$ 148,000	$ 150,000
REPAIRED:	$ 148,000	$ 150,000
30 AS IS VALUE:	$ 136,000	$ 138,000
LAND VALUE:	$ 24,000	

Value Range: $ 121000 – 159000
Land Value: $ 25,000
Repairs: $ 5,000

	Market Value	Suggested list price
AS IS:	$ 152,000	$ 154,000
REPAIRED:	$ 157,000	$ 159,000
30 AS IS VALUE:	$ 121,000	$ 123,000
LAND VALUE:	$ 25,000	

Value Range: $ 181000 – 183000
Land Value: $ 25,000
Repairs: $ 100

	Market Value	Suggested list price
AS IS:	$ 181,900	$ 182,900
REPAIRED:	$ 182,000	$ 183,000
30 AS IS VALUE:	$ 181,000	$ 181,500
LAND VALUE:	$ 25,000	

Value Range:	$ 129000 - 140000
Land Value:	$ 31,000
Repairs:	$ 5,900

	Market Value	Suggested list price
AS IS:	$ 132,100	$ 134,100
REPAIRED:	$ 138,000	$ 140,000
30 AS IS VALUE:	$ 129,000	$ 131,000
LAND VALUE:	$ 31,000	

Value Range:	$63000 - 101000
Land Value:	$ 15,000
Repairs:	$ 21,500

	Market Value	Suggested list price
AS IS:	$ 77,500	$ 79,500
REPAIRED:	$ 99,000	$ 101,000
30 AS IS VALUE:	$ 63,000	$ 65,000
LAND VALUE:	$ 15,000	

Value Range:	$ 115000 - 121000
Land Value:	$ 20,000
Repairs:	$ 1,000

	Market Value	Suggested list price
AS IS:	$ 118,000	$ 120,000
REPAIRED:	$ 119,000	$ 121,000
30 AS IS VALUE:	$ 115,000	$ 117,000
LAND VALUE:	$ 20,000	

Value Range:	$ 99000 - 107000
Land Value:	$ 15,000
Repairs:	$ 900

	Market Value	Suggested list price
AS IS:	$ 104,100	$ 106,100
REPAIRED:	$ 105,000	$ 107,000
30 AS IS VALUE:	$ 99,000	$ 101,000
LAND VALUE:	$ 15,000	

Visit www.Guide2BPO.com for
helpful resources and tools to
make your BPO business boom.